Top Skills

General Ability

For Selective Schools and Scholarship Preparation

Elyse Methven

A
FIVE SENSES
PUBLICATION

Five Senses Education Pty Ltd
2/95 Prospect Highway
Seven Hills 2147
New South Wales
Australia

Copyright © Five Senses Education Pty Ltd 2006
First Published 2006

Methven, Elyse
Top Skills – General Ability
ISBN: 978-1-741301298-8

Five Senses Education Pty Ltd
2/195 Prospect Highway
Seven Hills 2147
New South Wales
Australia

Methven, Elyse
Top Skills – General Ability
ISBN: 978-1-74130-129-8

How to use this book:

The tests are designed to prepare students for General Ability tests in Selective Schools and Scholarship Exams, helping them to think critically and expand their analytical and problem solving skills. This book can also be used to improve a student's general knowledge, problem solving and higher order thinking skills.

For the student...

When answering the practice questions, *do not simply guess* the solutions. This will not allow you to broaden your knowledge. Have a dictionary, thesaurus, encyclopaedia or the Internet nearby as tools of reference.

Remember that the questions vary in their degree of difficulty, and some are quite complex. Do not get frustrated if you cannot work out the answer. The questions are designed to test a range of abilities, and students will have strengths and weaknesses in different areas.

Students may time themselves while completing each test. However, it is important not to rush through the questions. Do not sacrifice accuracy for speed. Use the space provided at the end of the book to work carefully through each question. Drawing diagrams and pictorial representations may assist in finding a solution.

The extension problems located towards the end of the book are of a higher degree of difficulty. They have been engineered to challenge the mind and develop lateral thinking skills.

Tips for the exam ~

How to answer multiple choice questions:

- Read through the question very *carefully.*

- Think of a correct answer *before* the alternatives are given to you.

- If you cannot think of the correct answer, try and *eliminate* any answers that are unlikely or misleading.

- Read the four alternatives and choose the *best* or *closest* answer to what you think the question is asking.

- After choosing the best answer, *mark any difficult questions* so that you can come back to them if you have any spare time at the end of the test.

- *Attempt all questions.* You do not get marks taken off for answering a question incorrectly.

Remember to make sure you...

- *Plan and allocate time* for each question. For example, if the test is 1 hour and there are 30 questions; spend 2 minutes answering each question.

- *Do not waste too much time* answering any one question. Choose the best answer and go back to it at the end of the test.

- *Never rush.* Even if you think you know the answer immediately, read it through carefully to make sure you fully understand what it is asking.

General Ability Test 1

1. Circle the closest synonym of the word "subdued".

    a) hyperactive
    b) restrained
    c) insolent
    d) innocent

2. Baldeep has $4 worth of coins, made up of $1 and 20 cent pieces. He has 12 coins. How many 20 cent pieces does Baldeep have?

    a) 5
    b) 7
    c) 9
    d) 10

3. Meteorology is the study of:

    a) plants and flowers
    b) meteors and the planets
    c) weather and climate
    d) infectious diseases

4. The following numbers make a pattern. Fill in the missing number.

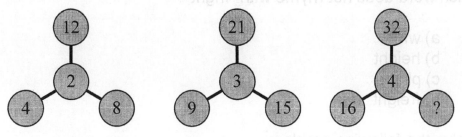

    a) 24
    b) 26
    c) 28
    d) 30

5. The country Thailand is located in which continent?

    a) Asia
    b) Australia
    c) Europe
    d) Antarctica

6. Which of the following three words is an antonym of "subtle"?

    a) complacent
    b) complex
    c) competent
    d) obvious

7. Carlos plays "Scissors, Paper, Rock" with Alex twice. How many different combinations can Carlos have? (Eg. 'rock then scissors' or 'scissors then paper' etc.)

    a) 6
    b) 9
    c) 12
    d) 16

8. Put these historical events in chronological order:

> The Moon landing, the first pyramid in Egypt is built, the internet becomes accessible to ordinary households, the First Fleet arrives in Australia.

_____

_____

9. Which word does not rhyme with "fright"?

    a) write
    b) height
    c) plight
    d) freight

10. Solve the following problem:

> lamb is to sheep as ..... is to horse

    a) foal
    b) hoof
    c) mare
    d) oxen

11. Circle the correct alternative:

> Marie Curie won the Nobel (Peace; Piece) Prize.

General Ability Test 2

1. Alicia competes in a race made up of tricycles and bicycles with 7 other competitors. If there are 21 wheels, how many tricycles are in the race?

      a) 3
      b) 4
      c) 5
      d) 6

2. Jansen picks out a number between 50 and 100. The sum of the two digits is 11. The product of the two digits is 28. What is the number?

_____

3. Hidden in CHEMISTRY is an antonym of "country". What is this word?

_____

4. Match the following words with their closest meaning:

Word	Meaning
emancipate	to free someone from personal, political, or legal restrictions
eccentric	acting with intent to deceive
fraudulent	blunt or curt in manner or speech
brusque	unconventional or odd

5. Who was Pablo Picasso?

      a) an early 20th Century Spanish artist
      b) a Mexican poet and philosopher
      c) the leader of the French Revolution
      d) the first man in space

6. Complete the following sequence:

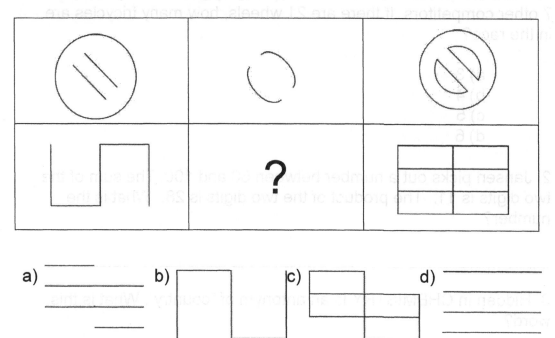

a) _____ b) (shape) c) (shape) d) _____

7. Yousof has a collection of 13 shapes made up of hexagons and heptagons. There are a total of 87 sides. How many heptagons are there?

  a) 5
  b) 6
  c) 7
  d) 9

8. Which words satisfy the following descriptions:

  a) An account of a person's life written by that person =
  An a _ _ _ _ _ _ _ _ _ _ _ _

  b) A animal that feeds on only plants =
  A h _ _ _ _ _ _ _ _

9. Which word can be rearranged to mean "blunt" or "straightforward"?

  a) credit
  b) centric
  c) dictate
  d) dialect

General Ability Test 3

1. Rachel has 7 less cherries than Nehal. Michael has 12 more cherries than Nehal. Nicholas has 4 times as many cherries as Nehal. Nicholas has 32 cherries.

        a) How many cherries does Michael have?

_____

        b) How many cherries are there altogether?

_____

2. What is meant by the following sentence?

> Today's politicians live in an ivory tower.

        a) Politicians live in white mansions.
        b) Politicians are down to earth people.
        c) Politicians must climb a colossal height to get to where they are.
        d) Politicians are not in touch with the realities of the modern world.

3. LARGE is to GIGANTIC as SMELLY is to ……..

        a) FRAGRANT
        b) ENORMOUS
        c) PUNGENT
        d) MILD

4. Which number does not belong?

> 16, 25, 36, 22

        a) 16
        b) 25
        c) 36
        d) 22

5. Hidden in SPELLBINDING is an antonym for "save". What is this word?

6. Place each of the following pronouns in the following table as either a "state", "city", "country" or "ocean":

Papua New Guinea, Indian, Melbourne, Arctic, Texas, Hawaii, Fiji, Victoria, Switzerland, Tasmania, Auckland, Seoul

state	city	country	ocean

7. The following numbers make a pattern. Fill in the missing number.

/4/—/14/
/1/—/2/

/8/—/28/
/2/—/4/

a) 5
b) 6
c) 7
d) 8

/12/—/42/
/3/—/6/

/16/—/?6/
/4/—/8/

8. Who was Alexander Graham Bell?

     a) the first president of America
     b) the inventor of the telephone
     c) an Austrian classical pianist and composer
     d) the inventor of the wheel

General Ability Test 4

1. Circle the correct alternative:

> My grandfather was (draughted, drafted) to serve in the Vietnam War.

2. Which word does not belong?

> woodwind, percussion, brass, saxophone

    a) woodwind
    b) percussion
    c) brass
    d) saxophone

3. What shapes can be used to make the following figure?

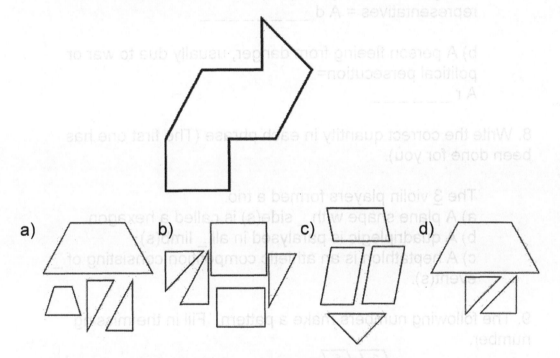

  a)   b)   c)   d)

4. Place the following words in alphabetical order:

> i) mess, ii) meander, iii) menial, iv) mesmerise

    a) i, iii, iv, ii
    b) ii, iii, i, iv
    c) iii, iv, i, ii
    d) ii, iii, iv, i

5. Which word can be rearranged to mean "less loud"?

    a) frostier
    b) florist
    c) forest
    d) defrost

6. Jasmine picks out a number between 10 and 70. The sum of the two digits is 12. The product of the two digits is 32. What is the number?

_____

7. Which words satisfy the following descriptions:

    a) A government by the people, or their elected representatives = A d _ _ _ _ _ _ _ _

    b) A person fleeing from danger, usually due to war or political persecution=
    A r _ _ _ _ _ _

8. Write the correct quantity in each phrase (The first one has been done for you).

    The 3 violin players formed a trio.
    a) A plane shape with _ side(s) is called a hexagon.
    b) A quadriplegic is paralysed in all _ limb(s).
    c) A heptathlon is an athletic competition consisting of _ event(s).

9. The following numbers make a pattern. Fill in the missing number.

    /3 /-/5 /
  /2 /-/4 /

    /3 /-/32/
  /5 /-/7 /

    /3 /-/45/   a) 0
  /6 /-/8 /   b) 5
                    c) 7
    /3 /-/7?/   d) 9
  /8 /-/10/

General Ability Test 5

1. What comes next in the following sequence?

AZ, CX, EV, ...

    a) FU
    b) GU
    c) HS
    d) GT

2. Ebony walks into a corner store. She buys one copy of "Dolly" magazine, a Snickers bar and a $1 can of Vanilla Coke. She hands the shop assistant $10 and receives $1 change. If the magazine costs 3 times as much as the Snickers bar, how much is the magazine?

    a) $4
    b) $5
    c) $6
    d) $7

3. Match the following words with their closest meaning:

Word	Meaning
breach	a frenzied emotional state
hysteria	to violate a promise or obligation
feasible	a position of superiority or fame
eminence	possible or able to be done

4. A faulty clock gains 2 minutes every hour. After 6 hours at school the clock reads 3:20pm. What time was displayed on the clock 6 hours ago?

    a) 9:04am
    b) 9:08am
    c) 9:20am
    d) 9:28am

5. Which word does not rhyme with "weight"?

    a) fete
    b) eight
    c) wait
    d) height

6. Find a number whose triple exceeds its quarter by exactly 44.

_____

7. What comes next in the following sequence?

V, X, XV, ...

    a) XVV
    b) VX
    c) XX
    d) C

8. Which of the following words is the class to which the others belong?

aluminium, metal, copper, iron

    a) aluminium
    b) copper
    c) iron
    d) metal

9. Solve the following equations:

    a) $12 - (4 \times [\ ]) = 4$

    b) $[\ ] \div 12 - 1.5 = 0.5$

    c) $6 \div 6 \times [\ ] = 2$

10. What 3-letter word can be added to the front of the following to form a larger word: "pet", "away", "bon" and "penter"?

_____

General Ability Test 6

1. Circle the correct alternative:

The continuation of the tennis match was (dependant; dependent) upon the weather staying fine.

2. Hidden in TELECOMMUNICATIONS is a synonym of "place". What is this 8-letter word?

_____

3. Each of the following shapes is reflected across the dotted line. Which shape's reflection will not be identical to the original image?

a)   b)   c)   d)

4. In what year did the First Fleet arrive in Sydney?

a) 1056
b) 1879
c) 1788
d) 1901

5. Place the following words in alphabetical order:

i) metaphoric, ii) metamorphic, iii) mentor, iv) metallic

a) iii, iv, i, ii
b) iii, ii, iv, i
c) iv, ii, i, iii
d) iii, iv, ii, i

6. In the acronym QANTAS, what does the letter Q stand for?

_____

7. Fin is travelling on a boat which slows its pace by 5km/h every 30 minutes. When she boards the boat at 9:00 am, the boat is travelling at 70 km/h. What speed is the boat travelling at 11:50am?

_____

8. In how many different ways can the letters ABCD be arranged?

    a) 12
    b) 16
    c) 24
    d) 48

9. Jonathan is sailing North from Australia to Papua New Guinea. He decides to turn his boat right. In what direction is he now travelling?

    a) east
    b) north east
    c) west
    d) south west.

10. Circle the closest synonym of the word "inevitable".

    a) modest
    b) dubious
    c) inedible
    d) certain

11. The following numbers make a pattern. Fill in the missing number.

    a) 1
    b) 2
    c) 3
    d) 4

General Ability Test 7

1. Anneke made a Lego seesaw. She put 10 blocks of Lego on the left hand side and 22 blocks of Lego on the right hand side of the seesaw. How many blocks of Lego need to be removed from the right hand side and placed on the left hand side so that the seesaw will balance?

       a) 6 blocks
       b) 7 blocks
       c) 9 blocks
       d) 12 blocks

2. Unscramble the following sentence:

> sky myriad the a scattered stars with night was of.

3. Which word does not rhyme with "chalk"?

       a) stork
       b) walk
       c) talc
       d) gawk

4. Write the correct collective noun in the space provided:

> deck, colony, flock, troop

       a) The gooey caramel was covered by a ………… of ants.
       b) A ………… of monkeys swung from tree to tree.
       c) A ………… of geese were flying south.
       d) The dealer shuffled out the entire ………… of cards.

5. Solve the following problem:

> Maori is to New Zealand as ………… is to Australia

       a) New South Welshman
       b) Canberra
       c) Uluru
       d) Aborigine

6. Which figure best replaces the question mark in the following pattern?

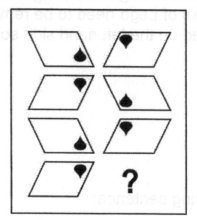

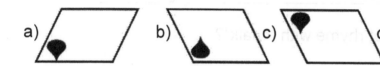

7. Which word can be rearranged to mean "dormant" or "inactive"?

        a) stinger
        b) grinner
        c) integral
        d) integrate

8. HUMOUROUS is to HILARIOUS as LOUD is to ……..

        a) SILENT
        b) HYSTERICAL
        c) DEAFENING
        d) MEEK

9. Which number does not belong?

56, 67, 28, 63

        a) 56
        b) 67
        c) 28
        d) 63

General Ability Test 8

1. Connie picks out one card at random from a pack of 52 cards. What is the chance that she picks out: (Write answers in the form of a fraction)

    a) A spade? _____

    b) A queen? _____

    c) A black card? _____

    d) A red king? _____

    e) A card that is not a diamond? _____

2. Circle the closest synonym of the word "callous".

    a) fallacious

    b) concerned

    c) cold-hearted

    d) amiable

3. Nadda, Connor and Yusef's birthdays add up to 19. Nadda's birthday is 3 times greater than Yusef's. Connor and Yusef's birthdays add up to 7. How old is each child?

_____

4. The following numbers make a pattern. Fill in the missing number.

    a) 3

    b) 5

    c) 6

    d) 9

5. If 8 gardeners take 16 hours to plant 32 trees, how many hours will it take 4 gardeners to plant 16 trees?

        a) 8 hours
        b) 16 hours
        c) 24 hours
        d) 32 hours

6. Write the correct quantity in each phrase (The first one has been done for you).

        The <u>3</u> violin players formed a trio.
        a) A dozen eggs is equal to _ egg(s).
        b) A monosyllabic word has only _ syllable(s).
        c) There are _ different event(s) in a pentathlon.

7. Which animal does not belong?

kangaroo, koala, emu, wombat

        a) kangaroo
        b) koala
        c) emu
        d) wombat

8. What comes next in the following sequence?

4, 2, 1, ½, ...

        a) 1
        b) ¼
        c) ⅛
        d) $^2/_1$

9. Which river is longer?

        a) The Murray
        b) The Mississippi
        c) The Amazon
        d) The Nile

General Ability Test 9

1. Fill in the missing number in Pascal's triangle.

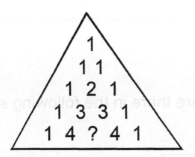

a) 3
b) 5
c) 6
d) 7

2. Hidden in PICTURESQUE is an antonym of "contaminated". What is this word?

_____

3. Brooke brings 8 oranges to cut up for her soccer team. She cuts the oranges into quarters. If each player wants only 3 quarters:

a) How many soccer players can she feed?

_____

b) How many quarters will be left over?

_____

4. Solve the following problem:

| hid is to hide as ………. is to eat |

a) eaten
b) eats
c) ate
d) eating

5. Which word does not rhyme with "brought"?

    a) naught
    b) taught
    c) draught
    d) thought

6. How many squares are there in the following shape?

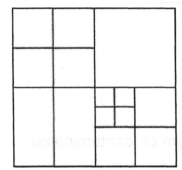

    a) 15
    b) 17
    c) 18
    d) 20

7. Place the following words in alphabetical order:

i) escapade, ii) eraser, iii) escapism, iv) escalator

    a) i, iv, iii, ii
    b) ii, iv, i, iii
    c) iv, i, iii, ii
    d) ii, iv, iii, i

8. Which word can be rearranged to mean "to feel pain"?

    a) beseech
    b) each
    c) teach
    d) beach

9. The fraction $^2/_8$ can also be written as:

    a) 0.1
    b) $^8/_2$
    c) 0.5
    d) ¼

General Ability Test 10

1. Who was Sir Edmund Barton?

     a) The first governor of Australia
     b) The first leader of the Democrats party in Australia
     c) The first settler in Australia
     d) The first prime minister of Australia

2. DISLIKE is to LOATH as LIKE is to ……..

     a) DETEST
     b) DISLIKE
     c) ADORE
     d) ABHOR

3. How many [shape] are needed to build the following shape?

     a) 9
     b) 10
     c) 11
     d) 12

4. Complete the following sentence:

     | A ………… is a doctor who works with children. |

     a) paediatrician
     b) optician
     c) statistician
     d) politician

5. Does a herring have feathers, fur or fins?

_____

6. Hidden in POPULATION is an antonym of "pleasure". What is this 4-letter word?

7. George had $4 in his wallet, made up of 10 cent and 50 cent pieces. He has 28 coins in his wallet. How many 10 cent pieces are there?

        a) 20
        b) 25
        c) 28
        d) 33

8. Alexa has 2 candles. Renée has triple the amount of Sasha's candles. Sasha has 10 less than Chad and half as many as Alexa. How many more candles does Renée need if she wishes to equal Chad?

_____

9. The following numbers make a pattern. Fill in the missing number.

/2/—/10/
/2/—/4/

/2/—/37/
/5/—/7/

/2/—/50/
/6/—/8/

/2/—/8?/
/8/—/10/

        a) 0
        b) 1
        c) 2
        d) 3

10. In which part of the body can the tibia be found?

        a) ear
        b) leg
        c) arm
        d) toe

11. Unscramble the following sentence:

In 1 World Zealand suffered Gallipoli losses heavy at and New Australia War.

General Ability Test 11

1. Solve the following problem:

> Said is to say as ………. is to shut.

    a) shutting
    b) shut
    c) shot
    d) shutted

2. If 5 painters can paint 10 rooms in 2 days, how long would it take 10 painters to paint 40 rooms?

    a) 1 day
    b) 4 days
    c) 10 days
    d) 20 days

3. Match the following words with their closest meaning:

Word	Meaning
emigrate	a person who pretends to be what he or she is not
compulsory	to leave one's native country to settle in another
benevolence	required by regulations or law
hypocrite	an inclination to do good or charity

4. Which instrument does not belong?

> bugle, trumpet, flute, trombone

    a) bugle
    b) trumpet
    c) flute
    d) trombone

5. Circle the correct alternative:

> The clerk wrote out a bank (cheque; check) for the lady.

6. Which word does not rhyme with "rough"?

       a) enough
       b) tough
       c) bluff
       d) dough

7. Sienna travelled around the world in 64 hours. She arrived at her destination at 9am on Thursday. At what time did she depart from her origin?

       a) 1am Monday
       b) 1pm Monday
       c) 5pm Monday
       d) 9am Tuesday

8. Circle the closest synonym of the word "sombre".

       a) senseless
       b) serious
       c) irrational
       d) sensational

9. The difference in distance between Lucy and Harry's house is 30 kilometres.

       a) If Lucy is driving at 120 km/h, how many minutes will it take Lucy to get to Harry's house?

_____

       b) Convert this into seconds.

_____

10. Hidden in INTERMEDIATE is an antonym of "calm". What is this 5-letter word?

_____

General Ability Test 12

1. Complete the following sentence:

A .... is skilled in making maps or charts.

    a) cartographer
    b) linguist
    b) osteopath
    c) chiropractor

2. Which figure should come next in the following sequence?

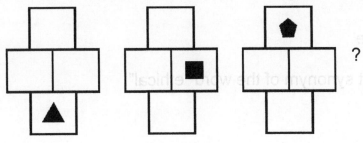

?

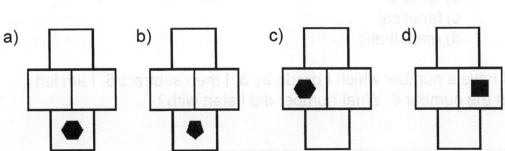

a)   b)   c)   d)

3. Find a number whose double exceeds its half by exactly 66.

_____

4. Write the correct collective noun in the space provided.

bunch, pride, pod, swarm

    a) The beekeeper was surrounded by a .... of bees.
    b) The florist handed the customer a .... of flowers.
    c) The scuba divers avidly followed a .... of whales.
    d) A .... of lions stood at the edge of the cliff.

General Ability Test 12

5. Circle the correct alternative:

> She decided not to go to outside because the weather was too
> (chilli; chilly).

6. Which colour does not belong?

> navy, scarlet, indigo, sapphire

      a) navy
      b) scarlet
      c) indigo
      d) sapphire

7. Circle the closest synonym of the word "ethical".

      a) moral
      b) farcical
      c) fanatical
      d) empathetic

8. I have a number which I divide by 3. I then subtract 5. I am left with the number 6. What number did I start with?

_____

9. Which of the following oceans or seas borders Australia?

      a) Atlantic
      b) Mediterranean
      c) Indian
      d) Arctic

10. Kelsey rolls a dice. What is the chance that he rolls an odd number?

      a) ½
      b) ¼
      c) ⅓
      d) ⅛

General Ability Test 13

1. Hidden in PATRONAGE is a synonym of "fury". What is this 4-letter word?

_____

2. Which is the largest in size?

        a) Earth
        b) Jupiter
        c) Pluto
        d) Mars

3. Complete the following sentence:

Malnutrition is predominantly caused by an insufficient ....

        a) knowledge
        b) patience
        c) sleep
        d) diet

4. Solve the following problem:

8 is to cube as ... is to rectangular prism

        a) 6
        b) 8
        c) 9
        d) 12

5. A farmer has a set of scales (drawn below) which he wants to balance. If the left hand side weighs 75 kilograms, and the right hand side weighs 59 kilograms, how many kilograms need to be removed from the left hand side and placed on the right hand side so that the scales balance?

        a) 3 kilograms
        b) 6 kilograms
        c) 8 kilograms
        d) 16 kilograms

6. Which words satisfy the following descriptions?

a) A person who designs buildings or other structures =
An a _ _ _ _ _ _ _ _

b) A medicine used to relieve pain or fever =
a _ _ _ _ _ _

7. Solve the following problem:

| Hearing is to deaf as ………. is to mute. |

a) sight
b) smell
c) taste
d) speech

8. Ivy's faulty alarm clock loses 2 minutes every hour. When her alarm clock goes off in the morning, it reads 6:30am. If Ivy set the alarm clock 9 hours ago, what time was displayed on her alarm clock when she set it?

a) 7:12 pm
b) 9:06 pm
c) 9:12 pm
d) 9:48 pm

9. Which of the following nets can form a triangular prism?

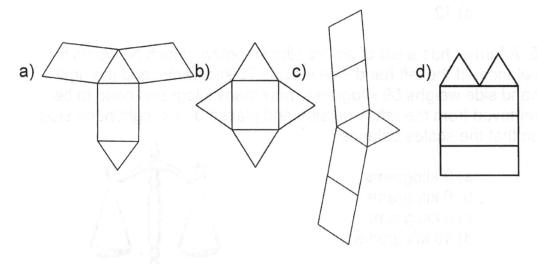

a)   b)   c)   d)

General Ability Test 14

1. Place the following words in alphabetical order:

i) yacht, ii) xenophobia, iii) xylophone, iv) xerography

   a) iv, ii, iii, i
   b) ii, iv, iii, i
   c) iv, ii, iii, i
   d) i, iv, ii, iii

2. Complete the following idioms:

   a) It's raining _____ and _____.
   b) The _____ bird catches the worm.
   c) Too many cooks _____ the broth.

3. Which word can be rearranged to mean "still" or "unchanging"?

   a) plastic
   b) attics
   c) caustic
   d) classic

4. What is the capital of the Northern Territory?

   a) Darwin
   b) Hobart
   c) Canberra
   d) Chatswood

5. By shifting the order of the letters...

   a) Change "lamp" into a type of tree.   _____
   b) Change "clam" into serene.   _____

6. What comes next in the following sequence?

1, 4, 9, 16, ...

   a) 24
   b) 25
   c) 26
   d) 27

7. Which word does not belong?

cautious, impatient, anxious, impulsive

    a) cautious
    b) impatient
    c) anxious
    d) impulsive

8. The following numbers make a pattern. Fill in the missing number.

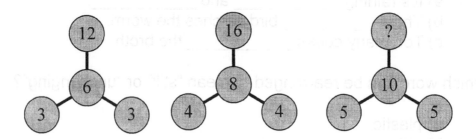

    a) 16
    b) 18
    c) 20
    d) 24

9. A grandfather divides $16 dollars into $2 and $1 coins for all of his 9 grandchildren. The children who are over the age of 5 receive twice as much as the children under 5. If the grandfather has no coins left over, how many grandchildren are under 5?

    a) 2
    b) 3
    c) 7
    d) 8

10. Which is higher: Mt Kosiosko or Mt Everest?

_____

General Ability Test 15

1. Which word does not belong?

transitory, lingering, prolonged, enduring

     a) transitory
     b) lingering
     c) prolonged
     d) enduring

2. Circle the correct alternative:

Many scientists people believe that (they're; there; their) is (too; two; to) much Carbon Dioxide being produced by humans (witch; which) contributes to Global Warming.

3. Complete the following sentence:

A practice used to reflect deeply on spiritual matters is called
....

     a) manifestation
     b) meditation
     c) mediation
     d) medication

4. In our solar system, which planet is closest to the sun?

     a) Earth
     b) Mercury
     c) Mars
     d) Venus

5. Charlie went on a trip to Canberra for a total of 55 hours. If he returned to Sydney at 4pm on Monday, at what time did he depart from Sydney?

     a) 9pm Friday
     b) 8am Saturday
     c) 9am Saturday
     d) 11pm Saturday

6. Hidden in LITERATURE is an antonym of "early". What is this 4-letter word?

_____

7. Does the tawny frogmouth have feathers, fur or fins?

_____

8. Write the correct quantity in each phrase (The first one has been done for you).

> The 3 violin players formed a trio.
> a) An octave is a musical interval of _ note(s).
> b) A unicorn is a mythical creature with _ horn(s).
> c) A musical composition for _ performer(s) is called a septet.

9. Match the following words with their closest meaning:

Word	Meaning
federal	more than is sufficient or required
superfluous	to find fault with or criticise
mentor	an advisor or guide
reprehend	a form of government where power is divided between one central body and several regions or states

10. If 4 chefs can bake 40 muffins in 10 minutes, how many minutes will it take 8 chefs to bake 24 muffins?

> a) 3 minutes
> b) 5 minutes
> c) 15 minutes
> d) 20 minutes

General Ability Test 16

1. Which figure should come next in the following sequence?

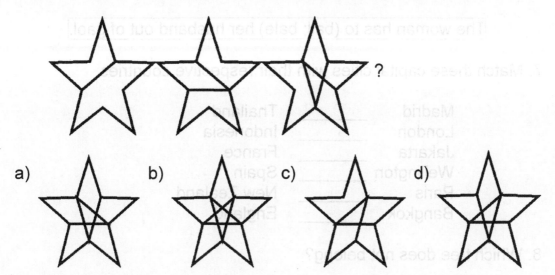

2. Who was J.R.R. Tolkein?

    a) a renowned Australian violinist
    b) a famous English novelist
    c) a French impressionist artist
    d) a 21st Century philosopher

3. What is meant by the expression "a close shave"?

    a) a jumbled getaway
    b) an intimate encounter
    c) a narrow escape
    d) a substantial haircut

4. Which word can be rearranged to mean "distant" or "isolated"?

    a) meteor
    b) metaphor
    c) metre
    d) metric

5. Lachlan picks out a number between 30 and 90. The sum of the two digits is 7. The product of the two digits is 10. What is the number?

_____

6. Circle the correct alternative:

The woman has to (bail; bale) her husband out of gaol.

7. Match these capital cities with their respective countries:

Madrid   _____   Thailand
London   _____   Indonesia
Jakarta   _____   France
Wellington _____   Spain
Paris   _____   New Zealand
Bangkok _____   England

8. Which tree does not belong?

wattle, jacaranda, eucalyptus, oak

a) wattle
b) jacaranda
c) eucalyptus
d) oak

9. What comes next in the following sequence?

i, ii, iv, viii, ...

a) ix
b) viiv
c) vv
d) xvi

10. Solve the following equations:

a) [ ] – 15 + (5 x 11) = 60

b) (7 x [ ]) – 4 = 24

c) 15 ÷ 3 + [ ] = 11

11. How many days were there in the year 1940?

_____

General Ability Test 17

1. Complete the following sentence:

A branch of medicine that deals with the skin is called ....

        a) criminology
        b) astrology
        c) dermatology
        d) oncology

2. What 3-letter word can be added to the front of the following to form a larger word: "verse", "fume", "cent" and "oxide".

_____

3. Find a number whose triple exceeds its half by exactly 50.

_____

4. Quinn had a collection of 9 shapes made up of pentagons and quadrilaterals. There are a total of 42 sides. How many pentagons are there?

        a) 3
        b) 6
        c) 9
        d) 12

5. What shapes can be used to make the following figure?

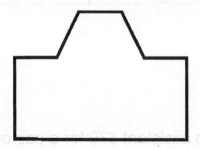

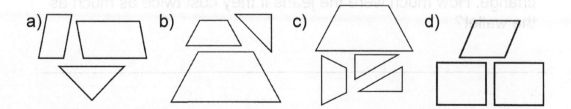

6. Place the following words in alphabetical order:

i) psyche, ii) pragmatic, iii) practical, iv) predominant

    a) i, iii, ii, iv
    b) iii, ii, iv, i
    c) ii, iii, iv, i
    d) iv, ii, iii, i

7. What is meant by the expression "to put on a pedestal"?

    a) to lift onto a high platform
    b) to idolise or worship
    c) to demonise or scold
    d) to ridicule or pity

8. Miranda starts at the library and walks 5 km south. She then turns left and walks 2 km east. She then turns left again and walks 3 km north and arrives at her home. How many kilometres south is Miranda's house from the library?

    a) 2 km
    b) 4 km
    c) 8 km
    d) 10 km

9. Which word does not belong?

compassion, forgiveness, pitiless, mercy

    a) compassion
    b) forgiveness
    c) pitiless
    d) mercy

10. Dakota gives a shop assistant $70 for a pair of Converse sneakers and a wallet. The shop assistant gives Dakota $10 change. How much were the jeans if they cost twice as much as the wallet?

General Ability Test 18

1. Circle the correct alternative:

> The doctor had (emitted; omitted) his middle name from the birth certificate.

2. By shifting the order of the letters...

        a) Change 'quads' into team.   _____

        b) Change 'drapes' into extend.   _____

3. In the middle column, write a word that comes after the word in the first column and before the word in the last column, to create two compound words:

Eg.	class	mate	ship
	sand	_____	back
	stop	_____	ripe
	nation	_____	wink
	data	_____	coat

4. Each of the following shapes is reflected across the dotted line. Which shape's reflection will not be identical to the original image?

a)   b) 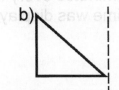   c) 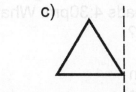   d)

5. What is a "catch 22"?

        a) a cricket term used when two players are caught out on the full

        b) a position which has both negative and positive aspects

        c) to strike a winner

        d) a no-win situation

6. Does a mackerel have feathers, fur or fins?

7. In how many ways can the numbers 1,2,3 be arranged?

        a) 3
        b) 6
        c) 8
        d) 12

8. Circle the correct alternative:

> The earrings perfectly (complemented; complimented) her outfit.

9. Which of the following words is the class to which the others belong?

> diamond, ruby, sapphire, gemstone

        a) diamond
        b) ruby
        c) sapphire
        d) gemstone

10. Ashleigh's defective watch gains 5 minutes every hour. After 8 hours her watch reads 4:30pm. What time was displayed on her watch 8 hours ago?

        a) 4:30 am
        b) 7:50 am
        c) 8:30 am
        d) 8:50 am

11. Write the correct quantity in each phrase (The first one has been done for you).

    The 3 violin players formed a trio.
    a) An octagon is an _ sided polygon.
    b) A decathlon comprises of _ different athletic event(s).
    c) An event which occurs every _ year(s) is called a centenary.

General Ability Test 19

1. Who was Mahatma Gandhi?

       a) a famous Hollywood actor in the early 1900s
       b) the inventor of sign language
       c) a peace activist for Indian independence
       d) a celebrated English poet from the Romantic period

2. What comes next in the following sequence?

> ab, ec, id, ...

       a) ad
       b) di
       c) of
       d) ou

3. Circle the correct alternative:

> The (principal; principle) put Lorenzo on detention for a week.

4. Which of the following words is an antonym of "mundane"?

       a) blissful
       b) doubtful
       c) invincible
       d) exotic

5. Jana rode her bicycle 44 kilometres to school from home. She then cycled ¾ of the way back to visit a friend. How far is Jana from her home?

       a) 10 km
       b) 11 km
       c) 30 km
       d) 31 km

6. Place these famous figures in chronological order based upon the historical time period in which they existed.

> Captain James Cook, Albert Einstein, Tutankhamen, William Shakespeare, Bill Clinton

_____

_____

7. Adam has $5 in his piggy bank, made up of 50 and 20 cent pieces. He has 19 coins. How many 50 cent pieces does Adam have?

a) 4
b) 5
c) 6
d) 7

8. Ena thought of a 4 letter word. The word has 3 letters in "seam", 2 letters in "pack", and 1 letter in "pink". There are no letters in "cusp". It starts with the letter "m". What is this word?

_____

9. Which word does not belong?

plate, wheat, trait, equate

a) plate
b) wheat
c) trait
d) equate

10. Solve the following problem:

7 is to week as ... is to fortnight.

a) 14
b) 15
c) 24
d) 52

11. What 3-letter word can be added to the front of the following to form a larger word: "ring", "mit", "bivore", and "ald".

_____

General Ability Test 20

1. Complete the following sequence:

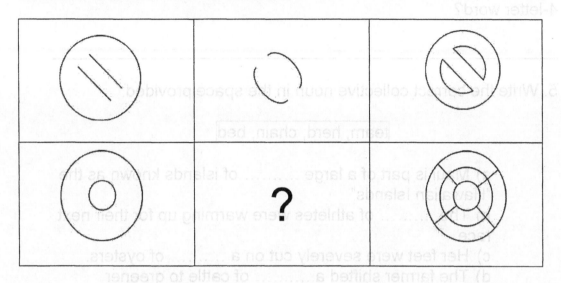

2. Which of the following words is the class to which the others belong?

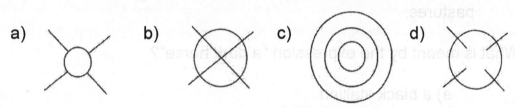

    a) zoologist
    b) teacher
    c) accountant
    d) profession

3. Anita's mother is twice as old as Anita. Anita and her mother's ages add up to 39. How old is Anita?

    a) 10
    b) 13
    c) 17
    d) 19

4. Hidden in COMPLICATED is a synonym of "friend". What is this 4-letter word?

_____

5. Write the correct collective noun in the space provided.

team, herd, chain, bed

a) Maui is part of a large ……… of islands known as the "Hawaiian Islands".
b) The ……… of athletes were warming up for their next race.
c) Her feet were severely cut on a ……… of oysters.
d) The farmer shifted a ……… of cattle to greener pastures.

6. What is meant by the expression "a dark horse"?

a) a black stallion
b) a malicious criminal
c) a person with hidden qualities
d) a lingering stranger

7. Which words satisfy the following descriptions?

a) A woodwind instrument with a single reed =
A c _ _ _ _ _ _ _

b) A person declared to be unable to pay his or her debts
= A b _ _ _ _ _ _ _

8. Find a number whose double exceeds its half by exactly 75.

a) 25
b) 40
c) 50
d) 75

9. Circle the correct alternative:

The boy's mother asked her son "Where did you (loose; lose) my mobile phone?"

General Ability Test 21

1. How many numbers between 1 and 40 are multiples of both 2 and 3?

     a) 6
     b) 7
     c) 8
     d) 9

2. Tracy rolls a dice. What is the chance that she rolls a 6 or a 2?

     a) ½
     b) ¼
     c) ⅓
     d) ⅛

3. How many triangles are there in the following shape?

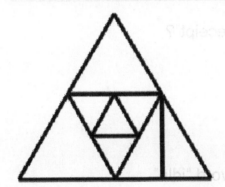

     a) 9
     b) 10
     c) 11
     d) 12

4. Which word can be rearranged to mean "discovered" or "studied"?

     a) crater
     b) nectar
     c) rental
     d) relate

5. Who is Nelson Mandela?

     a) The founder of the United Nations
     b) A South African leader and human rights activist
     c) A celebrated United States heavyweight boxer
     d) A Nigerian marathon runner

6. Match the following words with their closest meaning:

Word	Meaning
provoke	to stand or act aimlessly or idly
contaminate	to anger or infuriate
loiter	an exceptional interest in or admiration of oneself
narcissism	to make impure or to pollute

7. Unscramble the following sentence:

Michelle felt apartment her the trepidation dimly way lit into with.

8. Which word does not rhyme with "receipt"?

a) feat
b) replete
c) fete
d) conceit

9. Circle the closest synonym of the word "idle".

a) lazy
b) vigorous
c) confident
d) idyllic

10. Write the correct quantity in each phrase (The first one has been done for you).

The 3 violin players formed a trio.
a) A polygon with _ side(s) is called a quadrangle.
b) An octave is a musical interval of _ note(s).
c) A monologue is spoken by _ performer(s).

General Ability Test 22

1. Hidden in INTERNATIONAL is a mode of transport. What is this 5-letter word?

_____

2. Circle the correct alternative:

> She found a nine (carrot; carat) gold ring beside the letterbox.

3. Solve the following equations:

a) $9 \times 7 - 8 \times [\ ] = 39$

b) $[\ ] \times \dfrac{1}{4} - 0.5 = 0$

c) $(7 + [\ ]) \times 8 = 64$

4. The following numbers make a pattern. Fill in the missing number.

a) 4
b) 5
c) 9
d) 0

5. VITAL is to IMPORTANT as FURIOUS is to ……..

a) BALLISTIC
b) ANGRY
c) INSANE
d) SERENE

6. What is meant by the expression "a piece of cake"?

    a) a complex plan
    b) a slab of dessert
    c) a difficult endeavour
    d) an easy task

7. Who is Betty Cuthbert?

    a) An Australian television actress
    b) A track and field runner
    c) A contemporary poet
    d) The first female in space

8. Which word does not belong?

bat, stick, racket, ball

    a) bat
    b) stick
    c) racket
    d) ball

9. What 3-letter word can be added to the front of the following to form a larger word: "mi", "mary", "mons", "mertime"?

_____

10. Leighton has 6 red balls, 2 white balls, and 5 blue balls in a bag. He picks 1 blue ball out of the bag and doesn't replace it. He then picks a 2nd ball out of the bag.

a) What is the probability that the 2nd ball is blue?

_____

b) What is the probability that the 2nd ball is green?

_____

General Ability Test 23

1. Does a gazelle have feathers, fur or fins?

_____

2. Complete the following sentence:

A .... studies the earth's composition, origin, and structure by analysing rocks, minerals, and fossils.

    a) geologist
    b) ideologist
    c) zoologist
    d) cosmologist

3. Name the adjective in the following sentence:

The Internet has a vast array of sites to explore.

    a) Internet
    b) vast
    c) sites
    d) explore

4. Match the following words with their correct prefix:

truthful	dis
regard	in
ability	un
reliable	dis
conspicuous	in
content	un

5. By shifting the order of the letters...

    a) Change STAR into rodents.   _____
    b) Change ACRE into concern.   _____

6. Complete the following proverbs:

    a) A _____ in need is a _____ indeed.
    b) _____ speak louder than _____ .
    c) All that glitters is not _____.

7. Circle the correct alternative:

> She needs more (practice; practise) at tennis.

8. Hidden in RESTRICTIVE is a word meaning "to do your best". What is this 6-letter word?

_____

9. Find a number whose double exceeds its half by exactly 45.

_____

10. Write the correct quantity in each phrase (The first one has been done for you).

The <u>3</u> violin players formed a trio.
b) A pentagram is a star consisting of _ point(s).
c) A period consisting of __ year(s) is called a millennium.
d) There are _ day(s) in a fortnight.

11. What number comes next in the following series?

> 6, 18, 9, 27, 12, ...

a) 30
b) 33
c) 36
d) 39

12. Each of the following numbers is reflected across the dotted line. Which number's reflection will not be identical to the original image?

a) 8   b) 00   c) 44   d) 88

General Ability Test 24

1. Who was Florence Nightingale?

        a) A Hebrew prophet
        b) A classical Roman sculptor
        c) The first Australian female prime minister
        d) The founder of the nursing profession

2. Circle the correct alternative:

> The girl (brang; brung; brought) her puppy with her to the park.

3. Circle the closest antonym of the word "censor"?

        a) repress
        b) reveal
        c) cover
        d) sedate

4. Gregoire took a 45 minute bus ride to the beach. The bus was travelling at an average of 60 km/h. How many kilometres did the bus travel?

        a) 15
        b) 30
        c) 45
        d) 60

5. Does a Red Emperor have feather, fur or fins?

_____

6. What is ½ of ¼ of 28?

        a) 3.5
        b) 3.75
        c) 4
        d) 4.5

General Ability Test 24

7. Write the correct collective noun in each phrase:

colony; flight; chorus; belt;

a) A _____ of asteroids
b) A _____ of angels
c) A _____ of ants
d) A _____ of stairs

8. Solve the following equations:

a) $20 \times 10 - 50 \times [\ ] = 100$

b) $50 - [\ ] \times \frac{1}{2} = 35$

c) $33 \div (7 + [\ ]) = 3$

9. Complete the following sentence:

A .... is skilled in making maps or charts.

a) neurologist
b) dramatist
c) linguist
d) cartographer

10. If 6 painters can paint 36 rooms in 2 days, how long would it take 10 painters to paint 30 rooms?

a) 1 day
b) 2 days
c) 4 days
d) 6 days

11. Place the following words in alphabetical order:

i) honour, ii) honorary, iii) honourable, iv) honorarium

a) iv, ii, i, iii
b) ii, iv, i, iii
c) iv, ii, iii, i
d) i, iv, ii, iii

Extension

1. Soraya, Ali, and Rebecca each owned one pet; either a rabbit, a cat, or a dog. Each pet was a different colour; ether black, brown, or white. Rebecca's pet is not black and does not usually live in a cage or a hatch. Ali's pet is not a dog or a cat. Soraya's pet is white and not a cat. Who owned which pet?

Soraya   _____

Ali   _____

Rebecca   _____

2. Match the following inventors with their inventions:

Inventor	Invention
Alexandra Volta	sewing machine
Thomas Edison	automobile
Galileo	thermometer
Wright Brothers	battery
Henry Ford	aeroplane
Isaac Singer	electric lamp

3. Form a 7-letter word by using only the following letters.

INMU

_ _ _ _ _ _ _

4. What number is ½ of ¼ of ⅓ of 96?

   a) 3
   b) 4
   c) 8
   d) 12

Extension

5. The following numbers make a pattern. Fill in the missing number.

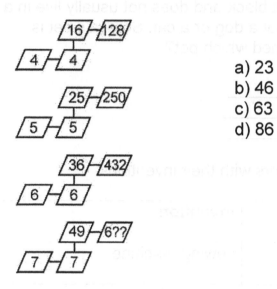

a) 23
b) 46
c) 63
d) 86

6. Penny leaves work and takes 5 hours to reach a town 60 km away. If she is travelling at the same speed, how long will it take Penny to travel from work to a town 80 km away?

    a) 6 hours 20 minutes
    b) 16 hours 20 minutes
    c) 6 hours 40 minutes
    d) 16 hours 40 minutes.

7. What sign can replace the question mark in order to correct this equation?

$12 \times 3 \boxed{?} (6 - 4) = 18$

    a) +
    b) -
    c) x
    d) ÷

8. Solve the following problem from the clues provided:

> I am not found in Australia. However, you can observe me near the start of Perth and at the end of Adelaide. I am never present in Spring or Autumn, but always present in Summer and Winter.

What am I? _____

Extension

9. Match the following countries with their respective capital cities:

Country	Capital City
India	Budapest
Finland	Abu Dhabi
Hungary	Islamabad
United Arab Emirates	New Delhi
Pakistan	Helsinki

10. Place the following events in chronological order

Women receive the right to vote in Australian federal elections; East Timor becomes an independent nation; The erection of the Berlin Wall; The opening of the Sydney Harbour Bridge; The massacre of student protestors at Tiananmen Square

1. _____   2. _____

3. _____   4. _____

5. _____

11. Unscramble the following words to form famous landmarks from across the globe:

JTA AMLAH   ___ _____

OUVLRE   _____

OCLOSSSU FO HRODSE _____ __ _____

OENENSHTGE   _____

PXHNSI   _____

UMACH CCHUPI   _____ _____

Extension

12. Solve the following problem:

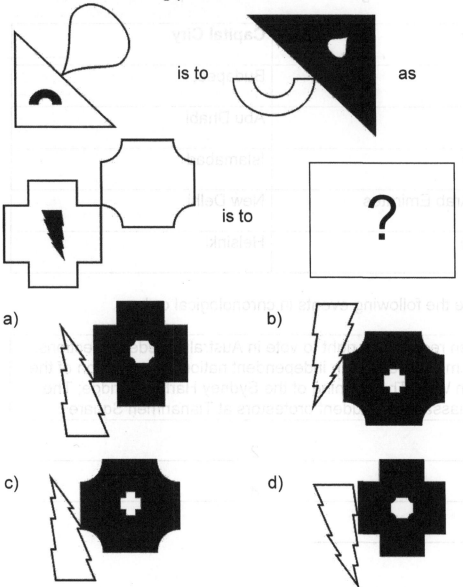

is to   as

is to

?

a)

b)

c)

d)

13. Which word is the closest antonym of "obstinate"?

     a) tenacious
     b) flexible
     c) abhorrent
     d) provocative

14. 0 is to READ, 1 is to ROGUE, and 2 is to RESOLUTION as ... is to ROSEWOOD.

     a) 2
     b) 3
     c) 4
     d) 5

Extension

15. Form a 6-letter word by using only the following letters:

$$\boxed{R \ E \ V}$$

_ _ _ _ _ _

16. A family weighs 235 kilograms altogether. The daughter weighs ⅓ of her father's weight. The mother weighs 20 kilograms less than her husband. The son weighs the sum of his sister's and mother's weights. How much does each person weigh?

Mother =	Daughter=
Father=	Son=

17. Which word is the closest synonym of "languid"?

    a) unbearable
    b) unenergetic
    c) unadorned
    d) unqualified

18. Circle the correct alternative:

The driver decided to let (loose; lose) and (flout; flaunt) her new car at the race (course; coarse).

19. How many numbers between 1 and 200 are multiples of 7, 2, and 3?

    a) 4
    b) 5
    c) 6
    d) 7

Answers

General Ability Test 1

1. b
2. d. (10 × 20 cents = $2) + (2 × $1 = $2). Therefore, there are 12 coins which add to a total of $4.
3. c
4. a. In the 1st set of circles, 2 × 2 = 4, 2 × 4 = 8 and 2 × 6 = 12. In the 2nd, 3 × 3 × 9, 3 × 5 = 15 and 3 × 7 = 21. And in the 3rd, 4 × 4 = 16, 4 × 6 = 24 and 4 × 8 = 32.
5. a
6. d
7. b Possible combinations are: rock scissors, rock paper, rock rock, paper scissor, paper rock, paper paper, scissors paper, scissors rock, scissors scissors.
8. 3100- 2950 BC: the first pyramid in Egypt is built (the Step Pyramid at Saqqara);
1788: the First Fleet arrive in Australia;
1969: the moon landing;
1996: the internet becomes accessible to ordinary households
9. d. The word "freight" rhymes with "late" or "hate".
10. a. Lamb is the young of a sheep as foal is the young of a horse.
11. Peace

General Ability Test 2

1. c. (5 × 3 = 15) + (3 × 2 = 6). 6 + 15 = 21 wheels.
2. 47. 4 + 7 = 11 and 4 × 7 = 28.
3. CITY
4. emancipate: to free someone from personal, political, or legal restrictions;
eccentric: unconventional or odd;
brusque: blunt or curt in manner or speech;
fraudulent: acting with intent to deceive.
5. a
6. a
7. d. Hexagons have 6 sides and heptagons have 7 sides. (9 × 7 sides = 63 sides) + (4 × 6 sides = 24 sides). 63 + 24 = 87 sides in total.
8. a) autobiography; b) herbivore.
9. a. "Credit" can be rearranged to form the word "direct".

General Ability Test 3

1. a) Michael has 20 cherries.
b) Nicholas has 32 cherries, Nehal has 8 cherries, Michael has 20 cherries and Rachel has 1 cherry. Hence altogether there are 81 cherries.
2. d
3. c. "Gigantic" is a stronger adjective than "large" as "pungent" is a stronger adjective than "smelly".
4. 22. It is not a perfect square i.e. 16 = 4 × 4; 25 = 5 × 5; 36 = 6 × 6.
5. SPEND
6. States: Victoria, Texas, Hawaii, Tasmania;
Cities: Melbourne, Auckland, Seoul;
Countries: Papua New Guinea, Fiji, Switzerland;
Oceans: Indian, Arctic.
7. a. In the 1st set of boxes, 1 + 2 + 4 = 7 and 7 × 2 = 14. In the 2nd, 2 + 4 + 8 = 14 and 14 × 2 = 28. In the 3rd, 3 + 6 + 12 = 21 and 21 × 2 = 42. In the 4th, 4 + 8 + 16 = 28 and 28 × 2 = 56.
8. b

Answers

General Ability Test 4

1. drafted
2. d. "Woodwind", "percussion", and "brass" are all sections of the orchestra, where as the "saxophone" is a woodwind instrument.
3. b
4. d
5. c. "Forest" can be rearranged to form "softer".
6. 48. $4 + 8 = 12$ and $4 \times 8 = 32$
7. a) democracy; b) refugee.
8. a) 6; b) 4; c) 7.
9. c. In the first set of boxes, $2 \times 4 - 3 = 5$. In the 2nd, $5 \times 7 - 3 = 32$. In the 3rd, $6 \times 8 - 3 = 45$. And in 4th, $8 \times 10 - 3 = 77$.

General Ability Test 5

1. d
2. c. The magazine cost $6, which is 3 times as much as $2.
$6 + $2 + $1 = $9. Hence Ebony would receive $1 change from $10.
3. breach: to violate a promise or obligation;
hysteria: a frenzied emotional state;
feasible: possible or able to be done;
eminence: a position of superiority or fame.
4. b. 6×2 minutes = 12 minutes. Therefore 3:20pm – 6 hours and 12 minutes = 9: 08am.
5. d. "weight" rhymes with "late" where as "height" rhymes with "site".
6. 16. $3 \times 16 = 48$. ¼ of 16 = 4. 48 - 4 = 44.
7. c. They are all roman numerals and multiples of five hence the next number in the pattern is 20 or "XX".
8. d
9. a) 2; b) 24; c) 1.
10. car

General Ability Test 6

1. dependent
2. LOCATION
3. a
4. c
5. d
6. Queensland
7. 45 km/h. At 11: 30am the boat has travelled for 150 minutes. 150 minutes ÷ 30 minutes = 5. 5×5km/h = 25 km/h. Hence the boat has reduced it speed by 25 km/h. 70 km/h – 25 km/h = 45 km/h. It will still be travelling at this speed at 11:50am.
8. c. There are 4 different letters hence the possible combinations are $4 \times 3 \times 2 \times 1 = 12$.
I.e. if A can occupy 1 of 4 positions, B can only occupy 1 of 3 positions, C can occupy 1 of 2 positions and D can occupy the only position left over.
9. a
10. d
11. d In the first set of boxes, $0 + 1 + 2 = 3$ and $3^2 = 9$. In the 2nd, $1 + 2 + 3 = 6$ and $6^2 = 36$. In the 3rd, $2 + 3 + 4 = 9$ and $9^2 = 81$. In the 4th, $3 + 4 + 5 = 12$ and $12^2 = 144$.

Answers

General Ability Test 7

1. a. 22 − 6 = 16 and 10 + 6 = 16. Hence there will be 16 blocks on both sides and the seesaw will balance.
2. The night sky was scattered with a myriad of stars.
3. talc
4. a) colony; b) troop; c) flock; d) deck
5. d. Maoris are the indigenous inhabitants of New Zealand as Aborigines are the indigenous inhabitants of Australia before European settlers arrived.
6. b
7. a. "Stinger" can be rearranged to form "resting".
8. c. "Hilarious" is a stronger adjective than "humorous" as "deafening" is a stronger adjective than "loud".
9. b. 67 is not a multiple of 7.

General Ability Test 8

1. a) ¼; b) $^1/_{13}$; c) ½; d) $^1/_{26}$; e) ¾.
2. c
3. Nadda is 12, Connor is 3 and Yusef is 4. Nadda's age = 3 × 4 = 12. Connor and Yusef's ages = 3 + 4 = 7. 12 + 3 + 4 = 19.
4. b. In the 1st set of boxes, 2 × 3 ÷ 2 = 3. In the 2nd, 3 × 4 ÷ 2 = 6. In the 3rd, 4 × 5 ÷ 2 = 20. In the 4th, 5 × 6 ÷ 2 = 15.
5. b. Each gardener takes 4 hours to plant 1 tree. Therefore if 4 gardeners can plant 4 trees every 4 hours, it will take them 16 hours to plant 16 trees.
6. a) 12; b) 1; c) 5.
7. c. An emu is not a marsupial.
8. b. Each number is being reduced by half.
9. d

General Ability Test 9

1. c. In Pascal's triangle, each number is the sum of the 2 numbers directly above it, hence 3 + 3 = 6.
2. PURE
3. a) 10; b) 2. There is a total of 8 × 4 = 32 quarters. If each player only wants 3 quarters, then 32 ÷ 3 = 10 remainder 2.
4. c. Hid is the past tense of hide, as ate is the past tense of eat.
5. c. "Draught" rhymes with "raft" where as "brought" rhymes with "sort".
6. c
7. b
8. b. "Each" can be rearranged to form the word "ache".
9. d

Answers

General Ability Test 10

1. d
2. c. "Loath" is a stronger adjective than "dislike", as "adore" is a stronger adjective than "like".
3. d. There are a total of 36 blocks in the larger shape. $36 \div 3 = 12$. Hence 12 lots of the smaller shape containing 3 blocks will make up the larger shape.
4. a
5. fins
6. PAIN
7. b. 25×10 cents $= \$2.50$. 3×50 cents $= \$1.50$. Hence $25 + 3 = 28$ coins, and $\$1.50 + \$2.50 = \$4$.
8. 8. Sasha has 1 candle, Chad has 11 candles, and Renée has 3 candles. $11 - 3 = 8$, hence Renée needs 8 more candles to equal Chad's amount.
9. c. In the first set of boxes, $2 \times 4 + 2 = 10$. In the 2nd, $5 \times 7 + 2 = 37$. In the 3rd, $6 \times 8 + 2 = 50$. In the 4th, $8 \times 10 + 2 = 82$.
10. b
11. In World War I, Australia and New Zealand suffered heavy losses at Gallipoli OR
In World War 1, New Zealand and Australia suffered heavy losses at Gallipoli.

General Ability Test 11

1. b. "Said" is the past tense of "say" as "shut" is the past tense of "shut".
2. b. Each painter can paint 1 room every day. Hence if 10 painters can paint 10 rooms per day, it will take them 4 days to paint 40 rooms ($40 \div 10 = 4$).
3. emigrate: to leave one's native country to settle in another;
compulsory: required by regulations or law;
benevolence: an inclination to do good or charity;
hypocrite: a person who pretends to be what he or she is not.
4. c. The "flute" is a woodwind instrument, where as the "bugle", "trumpet" and "trombone" are brass instruments.
5. cheque
6. d. "Rough" rhymes with "stuff" where as "dough" rhymes with "slow".
7. c. As there are 24 hours is a day, it was 9am Tuesday 48 hours ago. Another 12 hours ago (a total of 60 hours ago) it was 9pm Monday. And another 4 hours ago (a total of 64 hours ago) it was 5 pm Monday.
8. b
9. a) 15 minutes; b) 900 seconds. 120 km $\div 4 = 30$ km. Hence if Lucy travels 120 kilometres in 60 minutes, she will travel 30 km in 15 minutes as 60 minutes $\div 4 = 15$ minutes.
10. irate

General Ability Test 12

1. archaeologist
2. c
3. 44. $2 \times 44 = 88$ and $\frac{1}{2} \times 44 = 22$. $88 - 22 = 66$.
4. a) swarm; b) bunch; c) pod; d) pride.
5. chilly
6. b. "Navy", "indigo" and "sapphire" are all shades of blue, where as "scarlet" is a shade of red.
7. a
8. 33. As $33 \div 3 = 11$, and $11 - 5 = 6$. You can also work this problem out the opposite way, i.e. $6 + 5 = 11$, and $11 \times 3 = 33$.
9. Indian
10. a. A dice has the numbers 1 to 6 on each of its 6 sides. Hence there are 3 odd numbers; 1, 3, and 5. $\frac{3}{6} = \frac{1}{2}$.

Answers

General Ability Test 13

1. RAGE
2. b
3. d
4. b. There are 8 vertices on a cube, as there are 8 vertices on a rectangular prism.
5. c. $75 - 59 = 16$. $16 \div 2 = 8$. As $75 - 8 = 67$, and $59 + 8 = 67$, each side would have 67 kilograms on it and the scales would balance.
6. a) architect; b) aspirin.
7. d. A deaf person is unable to hear as a mute person is unable to speak.
8. c. 9×2 minutes = 18 minutes. 9 hours before 6:30am is 9:30 pm. 9:30pm – 18 minutes = 9:12pm
9. a

General Ability Test 14

1. b
2. a) It's raining cats and dogs;
b) The early bird catches the worm;
c) Too many cooks spoil the broth.
3. b. "Attics" can be rearranged to form the word "static".
4. a
5. a) palm; b) calm.
6. b. All the numbers in the sequence are perfect squares i.e. $1^2 = 1$, $2^2 = 4$, $3^2 = 9$, $4^2 = 16$, and $5^2 = 25$.
7. a
8. c. In the first set of circles, $3 + 6 + 3 = 12$. In the 2nd, $4 + 8 + 4 = 16$. In the 3rd, $5 + 10 + 5 = 20$.
9. a. If the children over 5 receive \$2 and the children under 5 receive \$1, and there are 9 children, then $7 \times \$2 = \$14$ and $2 \times \$1 = \$2$.
$\$2 + \$14 = \$16$.
10. Mt Everest. Mt Kosciusko is the tallest mountain in Australia, at 2.2 km above sea level. Mt Everest is the tallest mountain in the world; at over 8.85 km above sea level.

General Ability Test 15

1. a
2. there; too; which.
3. b
4. b
5. c. As there are 24 hours in a day (and 48 hours in 2 days), 48 hours before 4pm Monday is 4pm Saturday. Another 7 hours before that (a total of 55 hours ago), the time would be 9am Saturday.
6. LATE
7. feathers
8. a) 8; b) 1; c) 7.
9. federal: a form of government where power is divided between one central body and several regions or states;
superfluous: more than is sufficient or required;
mentor: an advisor or guide;
reprehend: to find fault with or criticise.
10. The time taken to bake muffins is independent of the number of chefs and the number of muffins. The time taken to bake the muffins is exactly the same i.e. 10 minutes.

Answers

General Ability Test 16

1. d
2. b
3. c
4. a. "Meteor" can be rearranged to form the word "remote".
5. 52. 5 + 2 = 7, and 5 × 2 = 10.
6. bail
7. Madrid: Spain;
Thailand: Bangkok;
London: England;
Indonesia: Jakarta;
Wellington: New Zealand;
Paris: France.
8. d. The oak is the only tree in the list which is not native to Australia.
9. d. The roman numerals are doubling each time. Hence double viii or 8, is xvi or 16.
10. a) 20; b) 4; c) 2.
11. 366. 1940 was a leap year, hence February had 29 days.

General Ability Test 17

1. c
2. per
3. 20. 3 × 20 = 60. ½ × 20 = 10. 60 − 10 = 50.
4. b. Pentagons have 5 sides and quadrilaterals have 4 sides. If there are 6 pentagons, then 6 × 5 sides = 30 sides, and 3 × 4 sides = 12 sides. 30 sides + 12 sides = 42 sides.
5. c
6. b
7. b
8. a. As Miranda has walked 5 km's south, and 3 km's north, 5 − 3 = 2 km. Hence her home is only 2 km's south of the library.
9. c
10. $40. $70 - $10 = $60, hence Dakota's 2 items cost her $60. If the wallet was $20, then the jeans cost twice as much i.e. 2 × $20 = $40. $40 + $20 = $60.

General Ability Test 18

1. omitted
2. a) squad; b) spread.
3. paper; over; hood; base.
4. b
5. d
6. fins
7. 6. There are a total of 3 numbers and 3 positions. If the number 1 can occupy 1 of 3 positions, the number 2 can only occupy 2 positions, and there is only 1 position left over for number 3. 3 × 2 × 1 = 6 different arrangements.
8. complemented
9. d
10. b. 8 hours ago the time would have been 8:30am. If the watch gained an extra 8 × 5 minutes (i.e. 40 minutes), 8:30am − 40 minutes = 7:50am.
11. a) 8; b) 10; c) 100.

Answers

General Ability Test 19

1. c
2. c. The 1st letter is the next vowel which follows alphabetically and the 2nd letter is the next consonant which follows alphabetically.
3. principal
4. d
5. b. ¾ × 44 km = 33km (i.e. if you break 44 km into 4 quarters, then 44km ÷ 4 = 11km. 3 of those parts is 3 × 11km = 33km). 44km – 33km = 11 km.
6. Tutankhamen: the king of Egypt around 1360 – 1350 BC.
William Shakespeare: an English dramatist and poet, born in 1564 and considered the greatest English playwright. Shakespeare wrote such plays as *Romeo and Juliet, A Midsummer Night's Dream*, and *Macbeth*.
Captain James Cook: an English naval explorer who, with botanist James Banks, sailed the *Endeavour* around New Zealand and the East Coast of Australia in 1770.
Albert Einstein: a German-born physicist who issued his general theory of relativity in 1915. He also worked on radiation physics and thermodynamics.
Bill Clinton: the 42nd president of the United States and member of the Democrat party, serving from 1993 – 2001.
7. a. 4 × 50 cents = $2. 15 × 20 cents = $3. $2 + $3 = $5.
8. make
9. b. "Wheat" does not rhyme with the other 3 words; "plate", "equate" and "trait".
10. a. There are 7 days in a week, as there are 14 days in a fortnight.
11. her

General Ability Test 20

1. d
2. d
3. b. If Anita is 13 years old, then her mother's age is 13 × 2 = 26 years old. 26 + 13 = 39.
4. MATE
5. a) chain; b) team; c) bed; d) herd.
6. c
7. a) clarinet; b) bankrupt.
8. c. 50 × 2 = 100 and 50 ÷ 2 = 25. Hence, 100– 25 = 75.
9. lose

General Ability Test 21

1. a. Between 40 and 1 there are 19 numbers divisible by 2 (38 ÷ 2 = 19). Of those 19 numbers; 6 (6, 12, 18, 24, 30, and 36 i.e. every 3rd even number) are divisible by 3.
2. c. As there are 6 faces on a dice, the chance that Tracy will roll wither a 2 or a 6 = $^2/_6$ = ⅓.
3. c
4. c. "Rental" can be rearranged to form "learnt".
5. b
6. provoke: to aggravate or infuriate;
contaminate: to make impure or to pollute;
loiter: to stand or act aimlessly or idly;
narcissism: an exceptional interest in or admiration of oneself.
7. Michelle felt her way into the dimly lit apartment with trepidation
8. c. "Fete" rhymes with "late" where as "receipt" rhymes with "meet".
9. a
10. a) 4; b) 8; c) 1.

Answers

General Ability Test 22

1. TRAIN
2. carat
3. a) 3; b) 24; c) 1.
4. a. In the 1st set of boxes, $(1 + 2) \times 3 = 9$. In the 2nd, $(2 + 3) \times 4 = 20$. In the 3rd, $(3 + 4) \times 5 = 35$. In the 4th, $(4 + 5) \times 6 = 54$.
5. b. "Important" is a weaker adjective than "vital", as "angry" is a weaker adjective than "furious".
6. d. Bats, racquets and sticks are all implements used in different sports such as cricket, tennis and hockey to hit balls.
7. b
8. d
9. sum
10. a) $^{4}/_{12}$ or ⅓ b) 0. At the start Leighton has a total of 13 balls in the bag. If he takes one blue ball out and doesn't replace it, he will have a total of 12 balls left in the bag, and 4 will be blue.

General Ability Test 23

1. fur
2. a
3. b
4. Untruthful; disregard; inability; unreliable; inconspicuous; discontent.
5. a) rats; b) care.
6. a) A friend in need is a friend indeed;
   b) Actions speak louder than words;
   c) All that glitters is not gold.
7. practice
8. STRIVE
9. 30. $2 \times 30 = 60$. $½ \times 30 = 15$. $60 - 15 = 45$.
10. a) 5; b) 100; c) 14.
11. c. The 1st, 3rd, 5th etc numbers in the pattern are increasing by 3. Every 2nd number is increasing by 9.
12. c

General Ability Test 24

1. d
2. brought. "Brang" and "brung" are not words in the English language.
3. b
4. c. 45 mins is the same as ¾ of an hour. Hence is the bus is travelling 60 kilometres an hour, $¾ \times 60 = 45$ km.
5. fins
6. ¼ of 28 (i.e. $28 \div 4$) = 7. ½ of 7 (i.e. $7 \div 2$) = 3.5.
7. A belt of asteroids; a chorus of angels; a colony of ants; a flight of stairs.
8. a) 2; b) 30; c) 4.
9. d
10. a. Each painter can paint 3 rooms a day ($6 \times 3 \times 2 = 36$). Hence in 1 day, 3 painters could paint 30 rooms ($10 \times 3 \times 1 = 30$).
11. a

Answers

Extension

1. Soraya: white dog;
Ali: black rabbit;
Rebecca: brown cat.
2. Alexandra Volta: battery;
Thomas Edison: light bulb;
Galileo: thermometer;
Wright Brothers: aeroplane,
Henry Ford: automobile;
Isaac Singer: sewing machine.
3. MINIMUM
4. b. ⅓ of 96 (96 ÷ 3) = 32. ¼ of 32 (32 ÷ 4) = 8. ½ of 8 (8 ÷ 2) = 4.
5. d. In the 1st set of boxes, (4 + 4) × 16 = 128. In the 2nd set of boxes, (5 + 5) × 25 = 250. In the 3rd set of boxes, (6 + 6) × 36 = 432. In the 4th set of boxes, (7 + 7) × 49 = 686.
6. c. Speed = distance ÷ time. Hence 60km ÷ 5 hours = 12 km/h. Speed ÷ distance = time. Hence 80km ÷ 12 km/h = 6 ⅔ hours or 6 hours and 40 minutes.
7. d
8. The letter "e"
9. India: New Delhi;
Finland: Helsinki;
Hungary: Budapest;
United Arab Emirates: Abu Dhabi;
Pakistan: Islamabad.
10. 1902: Women receive the right to vote in Australian federal elections,
1932: The opening of the Sydney Harbour Bridge,
1961: The erection of the Berlin Wall,
1989: The massacre of student protestors at Tiananmen Square
2002: East Timor becomes an independent nation.
11. TAJ MAHAL; LOUVRE; COLLOSUS OF RHODES; STONEHENGE; SPHINX; MACHU PICCHU
12. a
13. b. The number times the letter "o" occurs in each word.
14. b
15. REVERE
16. Mother= 55 kg, Father=75 kg, Daughter= 25 kg, Son= 80 kg. Using algebra, if we replace the father's weight with the pronumeral "a", then Father = a kg, Daughter= ⅓ × a kg, Mother = a − 20 kg, Son = (a − 20) + ⅓ × a kg.
If a + ⅓ × a + (a − 20) + (a − 20) + ⅓ × a = 235, then simplifying this equation gives 3⅔ × a − 40 = 235. To satisfy this equation, a = 75kg.
17. b
18. loose; flaunt; course.
19. a. Between 1 and 200, there are 28 multiples of 7 (200 ÷ 7 ≈ 28). Every 3rd of these 28 numbers is a multiple of 3 (28 ÷ 3 = 9⅓). Every 2nd of these 9 numbers is a multiple of 2 (9 ÷ 2 = 4½). Hence there are 4 numbers between 1 and 200 which are multiples of 7, 3, and 2.

Corrections

Corrections

Corrections

Corrections